My Country
Great Britain

Cath Senker

W
FRANKLIN WATTS
LONDON•SYDNEY

This edition 2013

First published in 2012
by Franklin Watts

Copyright © Franklin Watts 2012

Franklin Watts
338 Euston Road
London NW1 3BH

Franklin Watts Australia
Level 17/207 Kent Street
Sydney, NSW 2000

Dewey number: 941'.08612
PB ISBN: 978 1 4451 2701 9
Library Ebook ISBN: 978 1 4451 2413 1

Printed in Malaysia

Series Editor: Paul Rockett
Series Designer: Paul Cherrill
    for Basement68
Picture Researcher: Diana Morris

Franklin Watts is a division of
Hachette Children's Books,
an Hachette UK company.

www.hachette.co.uk

Every attempt has been made to clear copyright.
Should there be any inadvertent omission please apply
to the publisher for rectification.

Picture credits: Mike Booth/Alamy: 15t; David Burrows/
Shutterstock: 1, 6; Richard Clark/istockphoto: 2, 18; Roger
Cracknell/Alamy: 19; Kathy de Witt/Alamy: 7b; Empics/PAI: 5;
Gemenacom /Shutterstock: front cover cl, 4t, 7bl, 11bl, 15b,
17b, 21b, 22t; Granata1111/Shutterstock: 22b; David Hughes/
Shutterstock: 9; Gail Johnson/Shutterstock: front cover cr;
Liquoricelegs/Dreamstime: 14; Anthony McAulay/Shutterstock:
8; Ken McKay/Rex Features: front cover cl; Padmayogini/
Shutterstock: 11b, 24; Ina Peters/istockphoto: 10; rambo182/
istockphoto: 4b; Helene Rogers/Art Directors/Alamy: 13; Samot/
Shutterstock: 20; Iain Sarjeant/istockphoto: 3, 21; Homer Sykes/
Alamy: 12; Janine Wiedel/Alamy: 16; Willsie/istockphoto: 17.

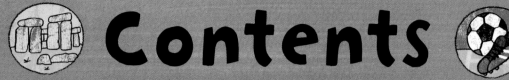 Contents

All words in **bold**
appear in the
glossary on page 23.

Great Britain in the world

Hi! My name is Jake and I come from Great Britain.

Great Britain is an island in Western Europe. It is a medium-sized country, made up of England, Wales and Scotland.

SCOTLAND

Edinburgh

Manchester

WALES

ENGLAND

Cardiff

London

Great Britain's place in the world.

Great Britain is one of the world's richest countries.

I live in Manchester, a big, important city in the north of England. We have two famous football teams.

Popular football team, Manchester United playing in red and white at their football stadium, Old Trafford.

People who live in Great Britain

A mix of British people at a London market.

Around 63 million people live in Great Britain. People from all over the world have made it their home.

Many come from the Caribbean, India, Pakistan and other countries.

Most people in Great Britain live in cities. The biggest city is the **capital**, London. It has more than 8 million people!

Nearly half of us live near the **coast**. Some people live in the countryside.

In the countryside, walking and cycling are popular.

My grandparents came to Great Britain from Ireland.

What Great Britain looks like

Much of the **landscape** is hilly with low mountains. In the east and south-east the land is flat. Around the long **coastline** are many beaches.

Scotland has many mountains, and it often snows in winter.

The countryside is covered in farmland. Around one-quarter of the land is used for farming.

Big cities like Manchester are packed with busy roads, homes, shops and offices. Our cities also have plenty of parks.

East Anglia, in eastern England, is flat and good for growing crops.

At home with my family

There are all kinds of families in Great Britain. Many children live with both parents. Some live with one parent or have a **stepfamily**.

Many families love playing electronic games.

We mostly enjoy entertainment at home, such as watching TV and playing on computers.

We also like to get together with grandparents, aunts, uncles and cousins.

I like going shopping with my family.

What we eat

In Great Britain, we like to eat meat, potatoes and vegetables, fish and chips, pies and sandwiches. We are fond of fast food, such as burgers and pizza.

People like eating fish and chips covered in salt and vinegar.

We have a choice of food from all over the world! British people adore curries, an Indian dish.

British people are also keen on sweet foods. We love cakes, biscuits and chocolate.

This family are buying a take-away meal to eat at home.

My favourite treat is chocolate cake. What's yours?

Going to school

Most children start school when they are four. I am seven, and I'm in Year 2. I'll go to secondary school when I am eleven.

At school, we do lots of drawing and painting.

14

The school day starts at 9am. We have a short lunch break. We all eat our lunch at school. Home time is 3pm.

Most children eat school dinners, but some bring a packed lunch.

At 3pm I go to after-school club until my parents finish work and pick me up.

 # Having fun

In our free time, we mostly have fun at home. We visit our friends' houses to play. Often, we go to the **local** park.

Adventure playgrounds are great for children.

In the holidays, some people travel to hotter countries to enjoy the sunshine.

Others take a break in Great Britain. They may go camping or visit the seaside.

When the sun comes out, people head for the seaside.

I love playing in the sand at the beach. The sea is very cold!

Festivals and celebrations

christmas is a christian festival, but everyone enjoys the holiday.

Our main **festival** is Christmas on 25 December. New Year on 1 January is a big holiday too.

In Scotland especially, people celebrate **New Year's Eve** with street parties and music.

On 5 November, people light bonfires and fireworks to celebrate **Bonfire Night.**

People of different religions celebrate their own festivals. For example, Muslims hold a delicious feast to celebrate **Eid ul-Fitr.**

Firework displays light up the sky on Bonfire Night.

Things to see

Most visitors to Great Britain head to London. The sights include Buckingham Palace and many museums. The London Eye ride offers fantastic views of the city.

On the London Eye you can see as far as 40km on a clear day!

Edinburgh, Manchester, Birmingham and Cardiff have many sights too.

Across the country are zoos, theme parks and castles. You can go on lovely walks around lakes and forests and climb hills.

Edinburgh Castle in Scotland attracts thousands of visitors.

I love visiting castles, although they can be creepy.

21

Here are some facts about my country!

Fast facts about Great Britain

Capital city = London is the capital city of Great Britain and England; Edinburgh is the capital of Scotland; Cardiff is the capital of Wales.

Population = 62,698,362

Area = 243,610km^2

Languages = English and Welsh

National holiday = Christmas Day

Currency = pound sterling

Main religions = Christianity, Islam, Hinduism

Longest river = River Severn (354km)

Highest mountain = Ben Nevis (1,344m)

Glossary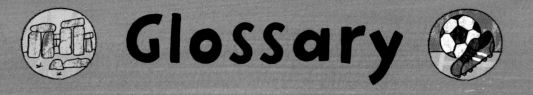

Bonfire Night the festival to remember when Guy Fawkes tried and failed to blow up the King and Parliament in 1605

capital the most important city in a country

coast where the land meets the sea

coastline the land along a coast

Eid ul-Fitr a Muslim festival to celebrate the end of the month of fasting (going without food for religious reasons)

festival a special time when people celebrate something

landscape what a place looks like

local to do with the place where you live

New Year's Eve the night before New Year

stepfamily the family formed when a parent marries again

Websites
www.bbc.co.uk/newsround/
CBBC Newsround. British news for children.

www.projectbritain.com/
Daily life in Britain. Includes homes, family, food and drink, and clothes.

Books
United Kingdom in Our World by Michael Burgan (Franklin Watts, 2010)

Country Files: Great Britain by C. Oliver (Franklin Watts, 2006)

Index